Wilson Reading System®
Student Workbook
Four A

THIRD EDITION

by Barbara A. Wilson

Wilson Language Training Corporation

www.wilsonlanguage.com

Wilson Reading System® Student Workbook Four A

Item # SW4A

ISBN 1-56778-085-7

THIRD EDITION (revised 2004)

The Wilson Reading System is published by:

Wilson Language Training Corporation
175 West Main Street
Millbury, MA 01527
United States of America

(800) 899-8454

www.wilsonlanguage.com

Printed in the U.S.A.

Read the word (hop). Write the new word with the **e** added (hope). Read the new word.

hop - e = _____   cap - e = _____

tap - e = _____   slid - e = _____

pin - e = _____   slop - e = _____

hid - e = _____   shin - e = _____

can - e = _____   cod - e = _____

Write all closed syllables in the closed syllable column. Write all **v-e** syllables in the **v-e** column. Read the words.

closed syllables		**v-e** syllables	
_____	_____	_____	_____
_____	_____	_____	_____
_____	_____	_____	_____
_____	_____	_____	_____
_____	_____	_____	_____

Underline each word. Mark the vowel with a macron (¯) and cross out the **e**. Read the words.

EXAMPLE: līm̶e̶

lime	quite	time
name	daze	rope
rake	pole	vote
line	broke	hose
shape	nine	flame
zone	smile	tape
stone	note	flute
game	choke	mine
drive	robe	safe
late	dime	like

Read each word below. Mark the short vowels with a breve (˘). Mark the long vowels with a macron (¯).

EXAMPLES: spĭt   crāne̸

note	shade	slush
take	spit	late
plate	hide	rake
hill	shake	step
sale	mash	life

Write the words above in the correct columns below.

words with closed syllables	words with **v-e** syllables	
_____	_____	_____
_____	_____	_____
_____	_____	_____
_____	_____	_____
_____	_____	_____

Underline or "scoop" each syllable. Write a **c** under the syllable if it is closed and a **v-e** under the syllable if it is vowel-consonant-e. Mark the vowels. Read the words.

EXAMPLES: <u>slĕd</u>   <u>shāke</u>
       c   v-e

smoke	step	white
chose	bone	scare
rash	snake	whip
five	prize	fire
spot	chimp	trade
crash	dish	slid
tape	hole	cloth
plate	cane	hope
rule	quilt	ride
ill	whale	tub

Write the vowel at the top of each box on the lines to correctly complete each word.

i	a
sh__ne	tr__de
wh__te	wh__le
dr__ve	w__ve

o	u
thr__ne	fl__te
sl__pe	pr__ne
st__ne	m__le

Write the words above on the lines below. Read the words.

_____   _____

_____   _____

_____   _____

_____   _____

Spell each word that is pictured.

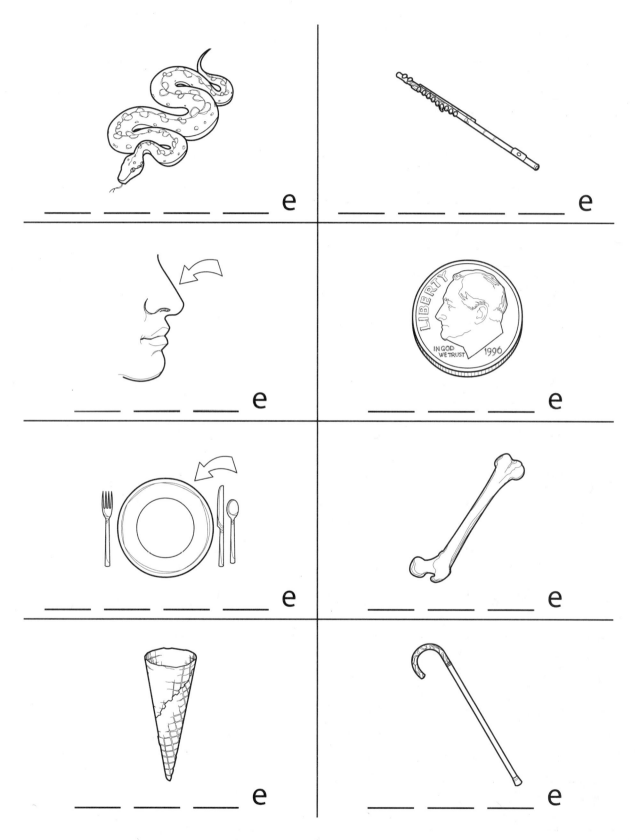

__ __ __ __ e

__ __ __ __ e

__ __ __ e

__ __ __ e

__ __ __ __ e

__ __ __ e

__ __ __ e

__ __ __ e

Underline all the vowel-consonant-e words in each sentence. Identify the syllables with **v-e** and mark the vowels. Read the sentence. Cover it and write it on the line. Uncover the sentence and proofread.

EXAMPLE: Kāte
       v-e

1 I like the cake and frosting.

_____

_____

2 I will rake the grass.

_____

_____

3 Steve fell in the hole.

_____

_____

4 Did Kate smile at that joke?

_____

_____

5 The whale came to life at last!

_____

_____

Read the sentence. Select the correct word from the box to complete the sentence. Write the word on the line. Reread the completed sentence. Use each word in the box only once.

white	snake	five	smile	safe
broke	chase	game	hope	flute

1 There is a _____ in the grass.

2 Alfred likes the red and _____stripes.

3 Ben was _____ at home plate.

4 Dad had a _____ and a wink for Tom.

5 I _____ that Jane is not late!

6 We can slide until _____ o'clock.

7 The pup did not _____ the cat.

8 Ned had a _____ and Dave had a trumpet.

9 Do we *have* time for a _____ of basketball?

10 Mike _____ his leg when he fell.

Read the words. Draw a line to connect the words that rhyme.

bikes	flaps
straps	strikes
rakes	bakes

hides	moles
holes	winks
blinks	tides

flakes	trades
skunks	bakes
grades	trunks

shines	pines
flags	ships
clips	drags

Select one word from each rhyming pair and write the baseword (without suffix **-s**) on the lines below. Read the words. Mark syllable type (closed or **v-e**).

_____   _____

_____   _____

_____   _____

_____   _____

_____   _____

Nonsense Words

Underline or "scoop" each syllable. Write a **c** under the syllable if it is closed and a **v-e** under the syllable if it is a vowel-consonant-e. Mark the vowels. Read the nonsense syllables.

EXAMPLES: <u>stŏt</u>　　<u>spīve</u>
　　　　c　　　　v-e

spive	stin	frot
stot	spad	frote
thrap	prete	zin
shike	blire	quib
thepe	chim	quile
drene	smip	steke
dren	spale	shope
swite	quate	drim
clem	guth	slep
quoth	fushe	triz

Combine the first syllable with the second syllable. Cover the divided word and write the word on the line. Uncover the divided word and check spelling. Read the written words.

cos - tume   = _____   bed - time   = _____

camp - fire   = _____   base - line   = _____

king - size   = _____   whale - bone = _____

ex - hale   = _____   in - clude   = _____

post - pone   = _____   frost - bite = _____

in - vite   = _____   dic - tate   = _____

clam - bake   = _____   flag - pole   = _____

hand - shake = _____   spare - ribs = _____

ad - mire   = _____   es - cape   = _____

class - mate = _____   con - crete   = _____

Read the syllables on each side of the box. Draw a line to connect syllables to form real words.

sun	cake
com	rise
cup	pare

vam	ball
mis	pire
soft	take

sun	fuse
ath	lete
con	shine

ad	ment
pave	side
in	vise

Write the words above on the lines below. Read the words.

_____   _____

_____   _____

_____   _____

_____   _____

_____   _____

Read the syllables on each side of the box. Draw a line to connect syllables to form real words.

hand	shake
king	pare
com	size

trom	pole
flag	mire
ad	bone

com	plete
base	pire
um	line

base	long
life	ribs
spare	hit

Write the words above on the lines below. Read the words.

_____   _____

_____   _____

_____   _____

_____   _____

_____   _____

Divide each word below into syllables. Read the word. Write the syllables on the lines.

explode   = _____ _____   flashcube   = _____ _____

concrete   = _____ _____   frustrate   = _____ _____

pancake   = _____ _____   reptile   = _____ _____

admire   = _____ _____   exclude   = _____ _____

milkshake   = _____ _____   pavement   = _____ _____

include   = _____ _____   baseball   = _____ _____

costume   = _____ _____   homemade   = _____ _____

postpone   = _____ _____   bedtime   = _____ _____

confuse   = _____ _____   drugstore   = _____ _____

compare   = _____ _____   classmate   = _____ _____

Underline or "scoop" the two syllables. Mark the syllables with a **c** or **v-e** to indicate syllable type and mark the vowels. Read the words.

EXAMPLES: <u>dis</u> <u>like</u>
      c v-e

dislike	vampire	sunshine
basement	whalebone	entire
extreme	stampede	spareribs
exhale	handshake	springtime
inside	invite	cupcake
collide	homesick	umpire
mistake	sunbathe	cupcake
flagpole	wildlife	concrete
hotcake	inside	athlete
compete	bedtime	unsafe

There are words spelled incorrectly in each sentence. They are underlined. Proofread and correct the words on the lines provided.

1   I hope that we can <u>escap</u> from this damp <u>cav</u>.

_____   _____

2   Let's *have* a <u>capcake</u> and milkshake.

_____

3   It is a shame that you <u>ded</u> not <u>invit</u> Steve and Kate.

_____   _____

4   Did you <u>drob</u> the <u>basebal</u> on the pavement?

_____   _____

5   The umpire <u>things</u> that Jane is a fine <u>athlet</u>.

_____   _____

Nonsense Words

Underline or "scoop" the two syllables. Mark the syllables with a **c** or **v-e** to indicate syllable type and mark the vowels. Read the nonsense words.

EXAMPLES: <u>căp</u> <u>sāte̸</u>
       c   v-e

capsate	inbefe	vilmite
trenzime	dispote	maseplod
transdope	exbale	vennape
conbrile	endame	filkipe
explobe	drenzime	plobbile
disfume	doselit	plebmat
poltrum	glibmax	fretjome
immone	laxtile	oppreve
drenvile	mentrabe	colgrone
pulvene	lebetrom	rettume

Combine the syllables to form a real word. Cover the divided word and write the word on the line. Uncover the divided word and check spelling. Read the written word.

dem - on - strate   = _____

con - tem - plate   = _____

post - pone - ment   = _____

con - trib - ute   = _____

rec - og - nize   = _____

in - com - plete   = _____

val - en - tine   = _____

tran - quil - ize   = _____

dis - trib - ute   = _____

Select the syllable at the top of each box that correctly completes the words below and write it on the line.

pone   com   tas
fan _____ tic
in _____ plete
post _____ ment

quil   trib   tab
es _____ lish
tran _____ ize
con _____ ute

con   lus   en
val _____ tine
il _____ trate
Wis _____ sin

og   trib   on
rec _____ nize
dis _____ ute
dem _____ strate

Write the words above on the lines below. Read the words.

_____   _____

_____   _____

_____   _____

_____   _____

_____   _____

Unscramble the syllables to form a real word. Write the word on the line. Read the word.

Wis   sin   con   = _____

nize   og   rec   = _____

lan   At   tic   = _____

plete   in   com   = _____

lus   trate   il   = _____

ball   bas   ket   = _____

tran   ize   quil   = _____

tab   es   lish   = _____

on   dem   strate   = _____

Underline or "scoop" each syllable. Mark them with **c** to indicate closed or **v-e** if vowel-consonant-e. Mark the vowels. Write syllables on the lines. Read the word.

illustrate   = _____ _____ _____

valentine   = _____ _____ _____

demonstrate   = _____ _____ _____

incomplete   = _____ _____ _____

contemplate   = _____ _____ _____

contribute   = _____ _____ _____

infantile   = _____ _____ _____

recognize   = _____ _____ _____

postponement   = _____ _____ _____

tranquilize   = _____ _____ _____

Read the sentence. Select the correct word from the box to complete the sentence. Write the word on the line. Reread the completed sentence. Use each word in the box only once.

demonstrate	valentine	distribute
postponement	recognize	

1 Mr. Cahill will _____ the test to the kids

2 Did Ted _____ the small pup

3 The _____ of the game upset Bill

4 The kids like to _____ the complex handshake

5 I think Chet gave Pam a _____

Write the 3-syllable words from the sentences above on the lines below.

_____   _____

_____   _____

_____

Underline or "scoop" any words with two or more syllables. Put a **c** or **v-e** under the line to indicate syllable type. Mark the vowels.

1 Mr. Jones will hire Dave to administrate the baseball camp.

2 Can you demonstrate that handshake?

3 We must get Jill to illustrate the script.

4 Steve can distribute the spelling test to the class.

5 Did you recognize that last song?

6 Mrs. Chang thinks that Dave contributes a lot in class.

7 Bob's infantile statement made his dad cross.

8 James must demonstrate his mistake on the math problem.

9 Kate was upset *about* the postponement of the game.

10 I would like to contribute to Mrs. Smith's fund for the homeless.

There are words spelled incorrectly in each sentence. They are underlined. Write the sentence correctly on the lines below. Add capital letters and punctuation. Proofread carefully.

1 we <u>liv</u> in Texas but Gabe <u>livs</u> in boston

2 Brad was <u>disruptiv</u> in math <u>clas</u>

3 steve <u>gav</u> jim a big <u>handshac</u>

4 Tom had <u>tin</u> dimes to get the <u>inexpensiv</u> gift for his mom

5 the <u>blak</u> <u>oliv</u> <u>fel</u> off the <u>plat</u>

Read the words below. Circle any word with a vowel-consonant-e exception (the final **e** is there for the **v** rather than to make the vowel long).

captive	impulsive	olive
expensive	incomplete	grapevine
inactive	live	have
admire	disruptive	escape
fantastic	inexpensive	active

Write the circled words on the lines below. Mark the syllable types.

EXAMPLE: c̆ăp tı̆vĕ
     c   v̶e̶

_____   _____

_____   _____

_____   _____

_____   _____

Read the sentence. Select the correct word from the box to complete the sentence. Write the word on the line. Reread the completed sentence. Use each word in the box only once.

disruptive	captive	olives	expensive	lives

1 I think James _____ in Wisconsin.

2 I did not like the black _____ in my salad.

3 The _____ child in class made Mr. Smith mad.

4 The kids held Dad _____.

5 That snack is quite _____!

Write the vowel-consonant-e exception words from the sentences above on the lines below.

_____   _____

_____   _____

_____

Review

Read the words below. Mark the syllables and the vowels. Be sure to mark vowels accurately in syllable exceptions.

blame	have	bind
give	mild	crime
cold	brunch	French
plant	brave	host
shade	blimp	lĭve or līve

Write the words from above into the correct columns below.

closed syllables	**v-e** syllables	exceptions
_____	_____	_____
_____	_____	_____
_____	_____	_____
_____	_____	_____
	_____	_____
		_____
		_____

Vocabulary Practice

Create sentences that include the vocabulary words below. Use a dictionary when needed. Underline or "scoop" each syllable in the vocabulary words.

4.1	4.2	4.3	4.4
trade	stampede	distribute	active
stale	inhale	contribute	expensive
shame	escape	demonstrate	disruptive
quite	include	postponement	captive
whine	postpone	incomplete	impulsive
share	compare		
brave	admire		
chase	invite		
daze	frustrate		
scrape	confuse		

Story Starter

At the end of Step 4, create a story that includes many (at least 5) of the vocabulary words below. This story is about a troublemaker. Underline each vocabulary word used from the list below.

disruptive	confuse	classmate	hope
compare	statement	contribute	name
escape	wildfire	entire	shame
intrude	dislike	chase	broke
pranks	distrust	punish	habit